FOLK DANCING
IN NORWAY

By
JOHAN KROGSÆTER

TANUM–NORLI
OSLO

Photos:
Norsk Folkemuseum, Bygdøy, p. 13.
P. A. Røstad Foto, Oslo, p. 14, 18, 21, 27, 29 and the coverpages.
Rådet for folkemusikk og folkedans, Trondheim, p. 23.
Teigens Fotoatelier, Oslo, p. 31, 32, 33, 34.

Drawings:
Ole Ekornes, Oslo, p. 10–11, 28, 30.

Front cover:
Folk dancing by the stave church from Gol at the Bygdøy
Folk Museum.

Translation by Brenda Koren
©Johan Grundt Tanum Forlag 1968
Second edition 1982
ISBN 82-518-1648-3
Mesna-Trykk A/S, Lillehammer

CONTENTS

INTRODUCTION

Norway is a country of contrasts. In the south the Long Mountains (Langfjella) divide it into East Norway—with its broad arable valleys, farming districts and sweeping forest-clad dales—and West Norway, with its countless islands, fjords, mountains and secluded valleys. The sheltered coastline and mild climate of South Norway are in marked contrast to conditions in other parts of the country, and the temperament of its inhabitants is also distinctive. North of Dovre lies the district of Trøndelag, its broad valleys bordering the Trondheim Fjord, and then comes expansive Hålogaland, stretching as far north as Latitude 71°, and as far east as the Russian frontier. The northernmost part of this area also borders on Finland, while the rest of Norway has a common frontier with Sweden.

Local cultural traditions vary from district to district, as the countryside itself changes. Many dialects are spoken, and Norway has no less than three official languages, "bokmål", with its origins in Danish, "nynorsk" (Neo-Norwegian), with its roots in Old Norse, and Lappish, spoken by a small minority in the extreme north.

One may draw a parallel between the dialects of a country's language and the variants to be found in its folk music. Generally speaking one can say that in Norway the folk music of the eastern part of the country is in a minor key, more so than in the west, and this distinction is reflected in the temper of the folk dances. The regional costumes of the east also have a distinctive cut to them. There could be many reasons for this, but probably the various routes of communications which linked the districts with other countries may have had a good deal to do with it.

Although Norway is situated on the northern fringe of Europe, strong cultural influences from the south and west have made themselves felt, in later years particularly from the United States of America. Gradually influence from abroad has become so strong that it has threatened to usurp much that distinguishes Norwegian culture. To counteract this, several organised movements are engaged in strengthening and nourishing as much as possible of the rustic heritage of the country. The work is carried on in the conviction that Norwegians would be impoverished as a people, and have less to contribute to the culture of the world as a whole, were they to lose their own distinctive national traits. The national authorities actively support this work in various ways.

NORWEGIAN FOLK DANCE

This is a general term for the old pair dances, regional dances, figure-dances and song-dances which constitute folk dancing in Norway. In connection with the song-dance, singing games and ring games may also be mentioned. The old pair dances include the Waltz, the Reinlendar, the Polka and the Mazurka.

The regional dances are five in number: the Pols, Springar, Rull, Gangar and Halling. Of these, the Pols and Springar possess similar characteristics and both are in Triple Time. The Rull, Gangar and Halling belong to one group, and are all in 2/4 Time (the Gangar and Halling also in 6/8). The Röros Pols is the best known of the Pols dances, but variations of the Pols are to be found in Österdalen, in Nordmöre, Tröndelag, Nordland and Troms.

The Rull, generally called the Vossarull, is particular to Voss in Hordaland.

The Halling or "lausdans" (literally "loose dance"—a solo dance performed by a male dancer) was previously danced in many districts throughout the country, but is now most common in Hallingdal.

The Gangar is to be found in three regions: in Valdres, where it is called "Opplandsgangar" or "Bonde" (bound), in Telemark and in Setesdal.

There are about twenty Springars, danced in most districts in South Norway.

Figure-dances are some sixty in number and can be grouped into Reels, "Feiarar" (of contra-dance character), Contra-dances, Quadrilles, etc.

The song-dance is also called the folk song game, as a great number of the songs used are old folk songs. The term folk song signifies those songs which have had an oral tradition extending over many generations and whose authors are anonymous. It is customary to divide the folk songs into "Trollviser" (Songs of Trolls), "Kjempeviser" (Songs of Giants), "Heilagviser" (Songs of

9

Hallingkast

Saints), "Riddarviser" (Songs of Knights), "Histo-riske viser" (Historical Songs), "Skjemteviser" (Humo-rous Songs), and "Dyreviser" (Songs of Animals). In addition there are many dances performed to folk songs of more recent date, and to the songs and lyrics of well known Norwegian poets and composers of our own time. A few song-dance lyrics are adaptations of Danish and Faroe originals.

THE ORIGINS OF THE SONG-DANCE

This dance form reached Norway about 1200. It came from France via England and the Western Isles (the islands of the North Atlantic), and was a Carol, consisting

of a lyrical stanza of four lines with a particular atmosphere of its own. After 1200, long narrative ballads
(which were danced) developed. A lyrical verse formed
the introduction, and part of this was repeated with each
successive verse, and became the burden or refrain of the
song. In this way the epic-lyrical dance-song came into
being. This fusion of lyrical and narrative song probably
took place in Norway or in the Nordic countries as a
whole, though apparently there has been a source of folk
song material common to the peoples of Northwest
Europe. Most of the foreign subject matter in the Norwegian folks songs has been transformed through independent creative talent, however, and has been colour-
ed in its new setting by local life, and by local beliefs and

11

attitudes of mind. Of specific Norwegian origin, however, are first and foremost the "Trollviser" (Songs of Trolls), which are based on Norwegian cultural traditions.

THE REVIVAL AND RENEWAL
OF THE SONG-DANCE

It is not known how long the song-dance of the Middle Ages remained popular in Norway, but it is believed to have died out in the eighteenth century. Reaching Norway from England, it spread to the Norwegian settlements in the west: Iceland, the Shetlands and the Faroe Isles. To-day it is only in the Faroes that the song-dance is still performed in its unbroken traditional form, and with this Faroe dance as its model the song-dance was reintroduced to Norway in 1902.

Hulda Garborg, the Norwegian authoress (1862—1934) initiated the revival of the song-dance. Subsequently, her work was carried on first and foremost by Klara Semb (1884–1970). It was on hearing Norwegian folk songs that Hulda Garborg was inspired to revive the song-dance. She first heard this kind of song in the 1880's, and was so fascinated that she determined to do something to preserve this cultural heritage, and to bring new life to the old folk song forms.

This, she thought, could be most effectively achieved through a revival of the old song-dances. Her knowledge of this old dance was at first scanty, but in 1901 she came upon a booklet, "Dans og Kvaddigtning paa Færöerne" (Dances and Lay Poetry of the Faroes) by a Dane, Hjal-

Hulda Garborg

mar Thuren, and with this to guide her she composed
dances to a number of simple songs. When, however, she
visited the Faroe Isles in 1902, she discovered that her
dance compositions had little in common with the Faroe
dances. The steps she had first taught have been called
"folkevisesteg" (folk song steps), but after her visit to the
Faroes she ceased to use them. They have, however, remained in some few dances, and will continue to live on
as an indication of how little Mrs. Garborg had to go by
when she started to revive the song-dance.

As a result of her visit to the Faroe Isles Hulda Gar-

Klara Semb (costume from Telemark)

14

borg began to use the Faroe steps known as "kvilesteg" (closed ballad step). At the same time, patterning the Faroe dance, she also introduced the "Ringbrot" (circle changes). It was not until the period between the two world wars that the Faroe "attersteg" (open ballad step) was danced in Norway, but it is now quite common. During the first years of the revival, dances were mainly composed to the epic folk songs, but gradually dance patterns were set to other songs too. From about 1920 Klara Semb began to compose dances to the poems and songs of such well-known Norwegian poets as Garborg, Vinje, Aasen, Sivle and Aukrust, and this led to an increased interest in the song-dance.

THE MUSIC OF THE SONG-DANCE

Most of the music of the folk songs used in the dance consists of old melodies whose composers are anonymous. Only a few folk song melodies are of more recent composition. Many of the newer folk songs have been danced to *folk tunes*. (Tunes, that is to say, whose composers are not known.) Most of the songs and poems written by well known authors of our own time have been set to music by contemporary Norwegian composers, though a few such songs are sung to music of foreign origin. The music of the song-dances is to be found in *"Norske Folkedansar I. Danseviser"*.

THE BASIC STEPS OF THE SONG-DANCE

The "kvilesteg" (closed ballad step) and the "attersteg" (open ballad step), both called Faroe steps, are the basic steps of the song-dance. Each step is divided into 6 beats of music: Left-Right, Left-Right, Right-Left. In dancing the closed ballad step, the movement is constantly forward, with the body turned in the direction of the line of dance. In dancing the open ballad step the dancers turn to face the centre of the circle, dancing clockwise two steps (Left-Right, Left-Right), and one step (Right-Left) counter-clockwise. The open ballad step has four tempi.

The "Folkevisesteg" (folk song step) is danced to songs with eight-beat music and is used only in a few dances. The dancers face the centre of the circle and dance clockwise Left-Right, Left-Right, and counter-clockwise Right-Left, heels raise, heels lower.

There are a variety of other steps, but these are generally used in the "Brigde".

Instructions for all the basic steps are to be found in the books, *Norske Folkedansar II*" and "*Danse-danse-dokka mi*" by Klara Semb.

THE ARM AND HAND HOLDS
OF THE SONG-DANCE

When dancing the closed ballad step, the *firm hold* is used. Each dancer places the right arm over neighbour's left. The right hand clasps neighbour's left in front of the thumb, and draws it close to the body where it is held

The "Kvilesteg"

The "Attersteg"

during the dance. The left arm is held close to the body with hands raised slightly above elbow height. The hold should be firm.

When dancing the folk song step the *free hold* is used.

Bandadans (Ribbon Dance) danced by people from the Faroe Isles

The men hold out their hands and the women place theirs on the backs of the men's with their fingers lightly clasping the palms inside. When dancing to the left the left arm is stretched out to the side and the right arm is bent under neighbour's left arm. The opposite is the case when dancing to the right.

When the *Faroe hold* is used to the *open ballad step* this is identical with the *firm hold*, but as the dancers in this case now stand facing the centre of the circle, the arms are held out from the body at about shoulder level. The underarms and palms of both men and women

18

should be held firmly. There should be no tensing of muscles and the elbow must be relaxed. These are the three most important holds of the song-dance, but not the only ones. There are others which will not be mentioned here. Most of them are used in the "Brigde" (variations).

"BRIGDE" AND THE OLD VARIATIONS IN THE SONG-DANCE

"Brigde" was not used in the original song-dance as we know it from the Faroe Isles. The variations known to us were "innbrot" (waving of the circle) and "snuing av rin-gen" (turning the circle inside out). Furthermore, in the Faroe "Sandoyar" dance partners were changed during the refrain. Men and women then joined each other and danced round on the spot, so that the man once more came into the circle on the woman's right when the refrain finished. This variation is used in the Norwegian folk dance "Han Mass og han Lasse". There were also two distinct forms of song-dance: a line-dance in which one row of men and one of women danced towards and away from each other, and the "Bandadans" (Ribbon Dance). In this the dancers stand in pairs in a line, each pair holding a ribbon between them. As the dance begins, the dancers lift their hands high and the couple heading the line turn towards each other and bending, move under the archway of ribbons until they emerge at the other end. Here they once more take up formation in the line which moves forward the whole time. This dance form is used in the Norwegian song-dance "Aka på isen håle", but with the added variation that the dancers join up and dance the last verse in a ring, but not in pairs.

At the outset of the song-dance revival it soon became apparent that one could not hope to achieve much unless the dance forms were made more varied than in the old ring-dances. Lengthy as they were and with contexts reflecting a far distant past, the old ballad songs were not suited to catch the interest of young people. For these two reasons new variations of dance patterns were set both to old songs and to songs and ballads of more recent years. These variations known as "Brigde" differ from the customary ring-dance with the Faroe step or other basic steps, and are usually danced during the refrain.

THE ORIGINS OF THE FIGURE-DANCES

The Norwegian figure-dances are of foreign origin, and probably reached Norway in the eighteenth century, some of them perhaps as early as the seventeenth century. Many of them probably came from England and Scotland, others from the continent. These dances must have been somewhat transformed after they arrived, and it is even possible that some figure-dances have been composed in Norway. We know for certain that much of the music of the figure-dances has been composed by Norwegian folk musicians.

Gamal reinlendar (Old figure-dance)

HOW THE FIGURE-DANCES WERE SAVED

It is chiefly to Klara Semb's credit that the figure-dances have been preserved. On her travels throughout Norway she wrote down approximately sixty dances of this kind. At this time some of them were no longer danced, but others remained popular until after the First World

21

War. It appeared that line-dances were to be found in East Norway and in Namdalen, whilst "feiarar" and reels were danced in many parts of West Norway, South Norway and Southeast Norway. Klara Semb taught figure-dances at the courses in folk dancing which she held, and directions for them were included in her books of instruction. She also published a collection of figure-dance tunes.

THE MUSIC OF THE FIGURE-DANCE

The music of the figure-dances originated abroad, but gradually Norwegian folk musicians composed original tunes. This was mainly due to the fact that it was customary for a fiddler to have at least one new tune in his repertoire when he played at a party. Shame on him who had not! So rather than be at a loss for a new tune he composed one himself. Many of the figure-dance melodies have been written down by Klara Semb and are to be found in "*Norske Folkedansar III*, Slåttar til turdansane" (Airs to the Figure-Dance). The music is written for the piano. There is also a collection of figure-dance melodies, "slåttar", arranged for the Hardanger fiddle by Henrik Gjellesvik, "Tonar til folkedansen" (Folk Dance Tunes).

THE ORIGINS OF THE REGIONAL DANCES

The Springar, the Gangar, the Vossarull and the Halling probably trace their origins to the early Renaissance dances. It seems that they were developed in Norway

Gangar from Setesdal

before 1600, and there is much evidence to show that they have been influenced by the song-dance which they supplanted. The Pols dances appear to have reached Norway in the seventeenth century. They came from Poland via Sweden and have replaced the Springar in the border country and northwards from Nordmøre.

TRADITIONAL AND NON-TRADITIONAL REGIONAL DANCES

The majority of the regional dances have an unbroken tradition. It is possible that some of them were in the process of dying out, but they were given new vitality when the organised movement to revive folk dancing was begun just after 1900. Here again Klara Semb was very active and accomplished much.

THE MUSIC OF THE REGIONAL DANCES

The "slåttar", the music of the regional dances, can be traced far back in time. There is evidence to show that the harp was played in Norway as far back as heathen times. Mention is made of the "fiðla" in the twelfth century and of the "gigja" in the thirteenth. One spoke of "slá fiðlu" (to strike the fiddle), and the use of the words "slått" (stroke) or "slag" (beat) for a dance melody, derives in this connection from the Norwegian verb "å slå" (to strike, to beat). It is difficult to say anything definite regarding the age of the Norwegian "slåttar", but examples such as "Förnesbrunen" (The Brown Horse of Förnes), "Kivlemöyane" (The Maidens of the Kivle Valley) and "Skjoldmöyslaget" (The Shield Maiden Air) date from the Middle Ages.

"Slåttar" for the regional dances are still composed, but the composers of the greater part of this kind of music are unknown to us. To a large extent the "slåttar" have been created by local folk musicians who have transformed and developed old material. This material has its origins in various parts of the world, and Norwegian folk music has followed scale patterns which for thousands of years were known to other peoples and used by them in their own music. The music of heathen times, however, was gradually supplanted as Christianity spread and the Church became a powerful factor in Norwegian rural society. To a certain extent the choral music of the Church has influenced instrumental folk music. The Vikings, too, must have been greatly responsible for bringing Norway into contact with the musical material and musical trends of other countries, for the most part those of France and England.

THE FOLK MUSIC INSTRUMENTS

The instruments of Norwegian folk music are: the Hardanger fiddle, the violin, the "langeleik" (Norwegian zither), the "seljefløyte" (willow flute), the "tussefløyte" (fairy flute), the "munnharpe" (the jew's harp), the "lur" (shepherd's horn), and the "bukkehorn" (goathorn). The clarinet, and various forms of violin have also been used in figure-dance music.

The Hardanger Fiddle.

This is a distinctive native instrument and the one that has played the most dominant part in the development of Norwegian folk music. The first Hardanger fiddles were probably made in the seventeenth century: the oldest fiddle of this type that we know of is dated 1651, and was made by Olav Jonsson Jåstad from Ullensvang in Hardanger. This fiddle may be seen in the Bergen Museum. It is deep and narrow, and much smaller than those in general use to-day. Furthermore, it has only two sympathetic strings, whereas the usual number nowadays is four. Not more than five sympathetic strings have ever been used. These strings are of steel and give a resounding drone when the upper ones are played. The Hardanger fiddle can be tuned in more than twenty ways.

The most usual are:

a) a----d---a----e   Raised Bass
b) g----d---a----e   Lowered Bass
c) a----e---a----c ♯   "Trollstille"

The Hardanger fiddle of to-day differs little in appearance from the normal violin, but the neck is somewhat shorter and the bridge flatter, and it is artistically decorated with inlaid mother-of-pearl, etc. It is played throughout large parts of Norway: in Valdres, Hallingdal, Numedal, Telemark, Setesdal and in West Norway as far as Sunnmøre.

The Hardanger fiddle

The "Langeleik"

is also a native instrument, probably dating from the six-
teenth century. It is mentioned in literature for the first
time in 1619. The strings are enclosed in a wooden case
with a sounding board. There is one melody string and
seven others, all of which are played upon. Under the
melody string are frets for the degrees of the scale. On
older instruments the scale patterns often differ greatly
from the usual European scale forms. When played the
"langeleik" lies on a table and the strings are plucked
with a plectrum. It can be tuned in several ways. In older
days this instrument was played throughout most of Nor-

27

The "Langeleik"

way, but nowadays it is most commonly used in Valdres where it is known as the "langharpe" (long harp).

The Jew's Harp

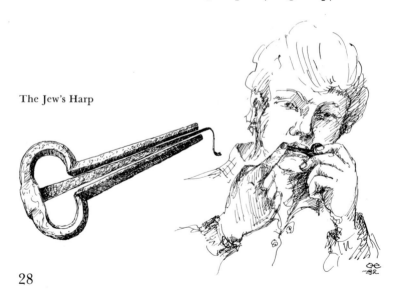

28

The "Seljefløyte"

is made of willow bark when the spring sap is running. It has a natural scale, and its best register corresponds to the overtones 7—16. The register may be doubled by closing the hole at the end.

The "Tussefløyte"

is of wood with a mouth-piece and finger holes. This instrument is also called the "sjöflöyte" (sea-pipe) and is a relative of the recorder. It is not native to Norway.

The Jew's Harp

came originally from Asia and was commonly used throughout Europe. It consists of a metal frame enclosing a steel spring. The frame is placed against the teeth and the free end of the steel tongue is plucked with the forefinger so that it vibrates between the teeth. The mouth is the resonator.

The "Lur".

The "Lur".

is a wind instrument made of two straight pieces of wood which have been carved out and bound together with birch bark to make a straight horn. Originally it was the instrument of the shepherds and shepherdesses. They used to play pastoral calls upon it to each other between the summer farmsteads in the mountains, as well as to the

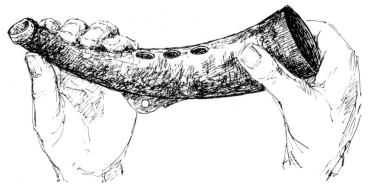

The "Bukkehorn"

cattle to call them home. When wild beasts threatened they played harsh frightening sounds upon it to drive them away.

The "Bukkehorn"

was used by the shepherds as a signal to call the cattle home, and also—like the "lur"—to frighten away wild animals. However, tunes can also be played upon it.

FOLK DANCE AND THE REGIONAL COSTUMES

There is a close connection between the folk dance and the regional costumes of the various districts. In Norwegian they are known as "bunader" (singular "bunad"), and unless they are worn by both dancers and musicians the folk dance lacks the right atmosphere. The majority of dancers and musicians wear the dress of the valley in which they live, or in which their families have their origins. Great importance is attached to the authenticity

30

Costume
from Hallingdal

Bridegroom's costume
from Valdres

of the costumes and to the propriety of manner with
which they are worn. First and foremost this means that
the "bunad" itself must be in accordance with the traditional style and set off by the correct accessories, i. e. the
head-dress, the apron, the right kind of stockings and
dark petticoat, and the black buckled shoes, the correct
shirt and the silver brooches and clasps. Suitable outer
clothing in keeping with the rest of the costume may also
be used, but nothing must be worn which destroys the
style of the "bunad" itself, and it must be worn with
dignity. There are also strict requirements as to the quality of the cloth, the needlework, cut, etc.

31

Wife's costume
from Hardanger

Costume
from Sunnfjord

It is believed that the regional costumes of Norway
have their origins in the costumes of the Renaissance, and
that they have been re-designed through fashion impulses
from abroad and through the independent artistic crea-
tions of country tailors and artists. This fusion of styles
has taken place over a period of several hundred years,
and the results reveal the great sensitivity to style of those
who have played a part in creating them. Not all the
regional costumes are strictly traditional. Many of them
have been re-designed on the basis of costume fragments
discovered in forgotten chests and cupboards, tucked
away in farmsteads throughout the countryside. The pic-

Costumes from Østerdal

tures and descriptions found in literature have also been a source of great help in this task of re-creation.

The liberal youth clubs, the domestic crafts guilds, the countrywomen's clubs and the women's institutes have been and still are the chief supporters of the movement for the revival of the "bunad". They have worked with praiseworthy energy to revive costumes which have gone out of use, to sustain a high standard of quality and a sound "bunad" tradition.

In an advisory capacity a national committee under the Royal Ministry of Family and Consumer Affairs gives its opinion and evaluation of all the regional costumes which are submitted to it and which it is the intention to

Costumes from Setesdal

bring back into general use. In addition there is a curator
of regional costumes at the Norwegian Folk Museum
(Norsk Folkemuseum) at Bygdøy, Oslo. Here, as at many
other museums throughout Norway, large numbers of
old regional costumes, or parts of such costumes, may be
seen.

There is a great variety of regional costumes in Norway, with women's costumes forming the majority. Not
only has each region its own distinct dress, but many
separate valleys have their own "bunad" too. This abun-
dance and variety indicate that in olden times there was
little intercourse among the country districts and among
the valleys.

The women generally have two costumes, one for everyday wear and one for festive occasions. The festival "bunad" is usually reserved for ceremonial and festive occasions of all kinds, and on May 17th, Norway's National Day, many Norwegians, especially women, may be seen wearing their festival costume.

The organised movement for the revival and preservation of the "bunad" dates back no earlier than to about 1900, and has gone hand in hand with the folk dance movement. Klara Semb has made valuable contributions in this sphere too. Apart from the war years, progress has been good in this field and there is nothing to indicate that it will not continue to be so. A comprehensive selection of books on the regional costumes of Norway is available. It deals particularly with women's dress.

FOLK DANCE AND NATIONAL REVIVAL

An organised movement furthering a Norwegian national revival was started in the latter part of the nineteenth century. Its main task was to re-establish Norway's national language as spoken in the rural districts. During the period of the Danish/Norwegian Union, which had lasted some four hundred years, the language of the joint administration and of the Church had become Danish, and Danish remained Norway's official language until the Union was dissolved in 1814. In the nineteenth century a growing national consciousness gave life to an organised movement promoting a national revival. It was felt that the language spoken in the valleys and other rural districts represented an unbroken linguistic—and indeed cultural —tradition and, therefore, should be reinstated as an official language.

The foundation for this "nynorsk" (Neo-Norwegian) was laid about 1850 by Ivar Aasen, and in 1885 the "Storting" (The Norwegian Parliament) decided that Neo-Norwegian should be adopted on an equal footing with the other official language. In this way Norway came to have two official languages which, over the years, have been influenced by each other so that the original distinction between them has by now been considerably diminished.

Hulda Garborg realised that there was a close connection between the Neo-Norwegian language on the one hand and Norwegian folk song, folk dance, folk music, and the regional costumes on the other. She started her work for the dance and the "bunad" in the "Bondeungdomslaget" (Country-Youth Club) in Oslo. This association had been formed to promote the re-establishment of the Norwegian national language, and to work for national independence in all spheres. Klara Semb continued Hulda Garborg's work, and saw clearly how the folk dance movement could contribute to the work of re-establishing the Norwegian language. She herself said that the driving force behind her work with the song-dance was the opportunity this gave her to win supporters for the language movement.

The folk dance movement is still an important part of the national revival movement, but folk dancing has also been performed in clubs which do not belong to "Noregs Ungdomslag" (The Youth League of Norway) or "Noregs Mållag" (the association identifying itself with the language movement). All the same, one is justified in saying that it is "Noregs Ungdomslag" which has charge of the development of the folk dance in Norway, and it is interesting to note that up to now no dances have been set to songs with texts in "bokmål" (the other official form of Norwegian).

FOLK DANCE TO-DAY

Folk dancing to-day is first and foremost associated with the Liberal youth movement, in other words with the individual clubs and branches of "Noregs Ungdomslag". The folk musicians, too, have their own organisation: "Landslaget for Spelemenn" (The National Association of Folk Musicians), which is very active in promoting the regional dances. Each year they arrange nation-wide competitions for musicians, and at these festivals large numbers of dancers take part in the competitions which are arranged for them as well. Regional competitions in folk dancing as well as local arrangements of this nature are also conducted in connection with contests for musicians. Folk dance competitions are also arranged by individual clubs of "Noregs Ungdomslag", but not too frequently, as it is the national festivals held at the time of the General Assembly that rouse the greatest interest and support. At these annual gatherings hundreds of dancers from all parts of Norway participate. The regional branches also hold annual meetings at which folk dancing is performed, and it is not unusual even for individual clubs to arrange festivals for great numbers of dancers. Moreover folk dancing is a popular feature of the clubs' activities, especially those which have their own folk dance groups (called "leikarring"). Public performances of folk dances have gradually gained a prominent place in the activities of these groups, particularly programmes for tourists. Public presentations of folk dances are, of course, somewhat inconsistent with the inherent nature of this kind of dance; but they have proved themselves to be of value in stimulating and strengthening the position of the folk dance to-day.

In addition to "Noregs Ungdomslag" and "Landslaget for Spelemenn", many other organisations concern themselves with folk dancing—temperance societies, for instance, and associations identifying themselves with the language movement. Certain political youth clubs as well as many schools are also active in this field. There are also folk dance groups sponsored by Folk Museums.

Norwegian folk dancers often travel abroad, and folk dancers from other countries also visit Norway. Inter-Nordic folk dance festivals are held every three years, and up to the present Denmark, Finland, Norway and Sweden have arranged these on a rotation basis. The Faroe Islands and Iceland have also been represented at these festivals, but have not as yet arranged such Nordic gatherings themselves. Norse festivals (Norse = Faroese—Icelandic—Norwegian) have, however, been arranged on the Faroe Islands.

38

The national authorities are favourably disposed towards the folk dance movement, and give financial support to travel, to the arrangement of international festivals and to the instruction of teachers for the folk dance groups. The Youth League of Norway holds annual courses for such teachers, and some forty delegates representing various organisations throughout the country take part. Courses for figure-dance musicians have sometimes been held simultaneously with those for folk dance teachers. A special council within "Noregs Ungdomslag" deals with matters relating to the folk dance groups, and a permanent course leader, who conducts courses in folk dance throughout the country, is a member of this council. Furthermore it is specified that each regional branch of the Youth League shall have a course leader responsible for the promotion of the folk dance in the district it covers. The number of courses held varies from year to year, but from 400 to 500 is not an unusual figure. This represents a total number of from 15,000 to 20,000 participants.

To a certain extent "Landslaget for Spelemenn" also conducts courses and receives financial support from the national authorities in this work for the regional dances and for the tuition of folk musicians.

On the whole it may be said that Norwegian folk dance is gaining in popular esteem, and that the movement for the preservation and revival of the folk dance is able to work under favourable conditions. In spite of this there are few people who participate in the folk dance as compared with the numbers of those who dance modern dances. There may be many reasons for this, one probably being that the folk dance movement is part of the movement for national revival which, in general, is most warmly supported by people whose roots are in country districts. If, nevertheless, the folk dance movement is numerically strongest in the towns, this is due in great part to the clubs comprised of people who have moved into the towns, which thus have the largest folk dance groups.

Programmes of folk dancing are sometimes televised, and the Norwegian State Broadcasting Company presents a regular half hour programme of folk music each Sunday.

The State Film Bureau has produced several films of instruction: "springar" from Aust-Telemark, "gangar" from Setesdal, "pols" from the Röros region, "springar" from Fana, "halling", "springar" from Jostedalen, "pols" from Nordmöre, "springleik" from Gudbrandsdalen and "halling" influenced by the tradition in Valdres.

An extensive collection of films is also available to the public at the secretariat of the Council for Folk Music and Folk Dance in Trondheim.

THE ACHIEVEMENTS OF THE FOLK DANCE MOVEMENT

During the comparatively short time it has existed, the organised folk dance movement has benefitted the national culture of Norway in various ways. When Hulda Garborg founded the movement at the beginning of the century, the song-dance was no longer danced. Many of the figure-dances were lost and some of the regional dances were on the point of dying out. An organised movement for the preservation of the regional costumes did not exist at all. The folk dance movement has given new life to much that was lost and forgotten, thereby saving a national heritage of great value. With the revival of the song-dance, many of the old folk songs were once more brought into the light, and became known to and treasured by young and old alike. The song-dance has also benefitted newer Norwegian literature, in as much as dances have been set to poems and songs by well-known contemporary authors. In this way thousands of people have become acquainted with and fond of a literature in which they otherwise might never have taken much interest. The fact that Neo-Norwegian literature has benefitted through the medium of the song-dance has also been of advantage to the language movement as a whole. Furthermore, through the widespread goodwill towards our national culture which the folk-dance has helped to generate, invaluable support has been rendered to the Neo-Norwegian language movement.

Folk dancing has been of great importance to codes of behaviour in social life. In circles where folk dancing is popular there is as a rule a propriety of manner and a tangible atmosphere of enjoyment that one seldom finds elsewhere. In many ways the song-dance may be said to be instrumental in releasing restraints, and through participation in the dance many a young person has been helped towards a freer and happier attitude to life in general. It has given them increased self-confidence, a broader outlook on life, an enriched capacity for receiving impressions and a consciousness of the value of their national culture. This has stimulated them to a wider range of activities, and in this way the liberal youth movement has gained many of its most enthusiastic supporters.

Both at home and abroad the folk dance movement has created great respect for the national culture of Norway, and has to a large extent had a stimulating effect upon the efforts of those engaged in the work for folk music and for the regional costumes. Nor can one rate too highly the opportunity it has given Norwegian children to express themselves in song and dance.

The Norwegian folk dance movement has not been introvert in its endeavours. It has to a large extent lived up to the ideals expressed by the great Norwegian poet, Olav Aukrust: "From the local, through the national, to the universal". An integrated network of international co-operation bears witness to this. Through international contacts, large numbers of young people have gained an insight into the cultures of many lands, and at the same time have spread far and wide a knowledge of their own national culture. The feeling of self-respect this has created, and the bonds of friendship that have been forged amongst folk dancers in many lands, are of great value.

AATTETUR FROM ASKER NEAR OSLO

Formation: Four couples in a ring, or a big ring of all dancers, the "free hold".

Steps: "Aattetur—step" a kind of walking step, but with a dip, a bending and stretching of the knees and ankles, twice on each foot in succession. Dip (bend and stretch) right knee lightly, step down forward on left toe, dip in left knee, lowering left heel until

43

touching the floor and dip once more while extending the body, step forward on right foot, toe touching the floor first. Continue as in walking steps.

Music 3/4: On each bar step down with a dip on the first count of the bar, raise on the second count again, dip on the third count and step down with the other foot on the first count of the next bar. In this way you step down alternatingly on left and right foot on the first count of each bar.

Tempo: Whole dance—one minute.

Music   **Dance:** *Figure I*. Ring (clockwise—counter-clockwise.) Start on
1—8   left foot, dance 8 "aattetur-steps" clockwise, turn on right foot,
1—8   keep hold, dance 8 steps counter-clockwise starting again with left foot.

Figure II, chain.
9—16   Partners turn face to face, join right hands and start chaining, women clockwise, men counter-clockwise, using "aatteturstep". Chain until meeting own partner (8 steps), turn around so as to change place with 2 steps, right arms in a high arch, women hold out skirts with left hand, men left hand low on hip, and then
9—16   chain back, women now C—C, men C. Stop in front of partner without joining hands. If danced with more than four couples, chain to fifth dancer (own partner included), turn with him and chain back.

Figure III. Curtsey and waltz.
Men cross arms over chest and bow to their partners. At the
17—32 same time women hold their skirts out to side with both hands, placing left foot behind right, bending, head forward, keeping back straight, drop directly down until left knee touches the floor. Then rise slowly and close left foot to right. Raise head last.

Men place hands on partners' waists, women place hands on partners' shoulders. Dance 12 waltz steps (couples clockwise, but the whole ring moves counter-clockwise). Open hold and make a light curtsey on the two last beats of the music.

44

SWEEPER (FEIAR)

Formation: Couples behind each other in ring counter-clockwise. Men give right hands to left hands of the women. They both place the other hand on the hip with thumb forwards.

Tempo: Whole dance—20 seconds.

Begin with outside foot, left for men, right for women and dance 3 two-steps turning face to face and back to back for each step. When partners are facing each other the hands are swung backwards and when they are back to back the hands are swung forward. Then turn with two walking steps with stamp. Change hand. Men begin with right and women with left foot and dance 3 twosteps in the opposite direction and stop with two walking steps with stamp. Couple I turns rapidly towards Couple II, all clap hands, join right hands, and form a mill with the thumb grip. All begin with left foot and dance 8 hop steps, clockwise. Let hand grip go, clap hands, change hand, begin with left foot and dance 8 hop steps counter-clockwise. Then change places as follows: When the mill stops, man in Couple II gives his left hand to right hand of his partner forming an arch turned towards Couple I. Man in Couple I gives his right hand to left hand of his partner. Couple I begins dancing two-steps. Man with left, woman with right foot go under the arch on first step and dance further 2 two-steps until they turn with stamp on two walking steps. Couple

1—4

1—4

5—8

5—8

45

II begins at the same time, man with left foot and woman with right foot and dance one two-step towards Couple I who goes under the arch. Then Couple II turns rapidly, man on left foot and woman on right foot, changes hands and follows after Couple I and dances first figure as described above. Then Couple II stops and Couple I turns to dance a mill once more, each time with a new couple.

BENDIK AND AAROLILJA*)

Ingvar Bøhn

Bendik rode to Selondo
There a Maiden to find.
But oh alas, he shall ne'er come back,
Cruel fate has doomed him to die.
Refrain: Aarolilja, why do you sleep so long?

*) Translated by Mabel Shirley, St. Olaf College, Northfield, Minn.

46

Bendik dwelt in the castle,
But ere he a fortnight was there
He fell in love with the Kings's own daughter,
A Maiden so young and fair.

The King he built a draw-bridge high,
Built it of shining gold.
"Whoever crosses this bridge shall die
Be he a prince or a warrior bold."

Answered young Bendik boldly,
Fear was not in his heart:
"I shall cross your bridge of gold
Tho' with my life I must part."

All through the day young Bendik rides
Hunting the swift running deer.
But with the night he comes again
The lovely Maid to be near.

Bendik tells her of his love,
Praises her beauty rare:
"Like ripe yellow apples bending low
Are the braids of your golden hair."

Listening near the King's young page
Hastened the message to bring:
"Young Bendik has crossed the golden bridge
Disobeying the word of the King."

Down came the fist of the Danish King:
"For this young Bendik shall die,
And ne'er the riches of all the world
Shall pardon for Bendik buy."

47

Shadow fell on the whole wide world,
All things his sorrow shared:
The birds and the leaves and the quiet deer,
All begged that his life be spared.

Kneeling before the angry King
Bows Aarolilja to pray:
"Oh, father, dear, pray spare my love,
Oh spare my love for me."

"I do not hear your pleading fine,
Leave me lest I forget
How evil it would be if this sword of mine
With a woman's blood got wet".

There beside the lonely church
Bendik they cruelly slayed,
And high in the tower she pined away
That broken-hearted maid.

On either side of the lonely church
In sleep rest those lovers of old,
And out of their graves two lilies grow
So wonderful to behold.

High o'er the tower the lilies grow,
To each other they cling
And ever as they twine on high
They mark the doom of the King.
Aarolilja, why do you sleep so long?

BENDIK AND AAROLILJA

Formation: Ring with the "Firm Hold".
Steps: "Closed Ballad Steps".
Rhythm: Ben-dik rode to Selondo.
  1   2   3   4 5   6   1 2

48

Tempo: The tempo of song and movements is accelerated or decelerated according to the dramatic content of the ballad. Start rather quickly, otherwise the ending will be too slow.

The Dance:

Dance 5 closed ballad steps, singing the whole stanza exclusive of the refrain. On the two last beats of the 5th step turn towards center of the ring and take last step inwards, the men take a little longer step in order to get in front of the women. Lower arms and release the hold.

Bars. 1—8

The men slowly join hands in front of the women. With body weight on right foot, bend right knee and upper part of the body slightly, then stretch out again, lifting arms forward and upward, stepping backward on left foot. Close right foot to left foot, lowering arms slowly again. The movement must be gliding, the arms drawing a circle. Bend right knee on "Aaro" step backward on "lil" and close right foot to left foot on "ja".

8—9

The women at the same time bend low forward, taking a short step forward on left foot under the arches formed by the arms of the men, then they rise slowly up and close right foot to left joining hands in front of the men.

8—9

The women then take a step backward in the same way as described for the men under bars 8—9 at the same time as *the men* step forward under the arches of the arms of the women as described for the women in bars 8—9, all singing "why do you sleep".

9—10

The men finally, step backward and *the women* forward again, changing places in the same way once more, all singing "so long".

10—11

The women do not join hands after stepping forward into the ring the last time.

The men keep the hold until next stanza starts.

The movement symbolizes a lily blossom opening and closing. The name Aarolilja means beautiful lily.

The refrain of the stanza is danced differently.

8—11

The men bend the upper part of the body slightly forward

49

extend hands sideways—downward, place palm to palm of partner, in front of the women. They then raise their arms very slowly
inward and upward, at the same time stretching the upper body
until arms are pointing upward, straight but not stiff, and the
body is slightly curved backward. Eyes follow the arm movement.
The arms are moved so slowly that they exactly follow the words
of the refrain and they do not reach the final position before the
last word is sung.

8—11   *The women* cross arms over their chests, bending their heads.
They remain in this position until the refrain is sung.

The men slowly lower arms and release hold, the women lower
arms and men and women simultaneously take up a natural standing position.

STRIVE FOR PEACE

Sparre Olsen.

With faith to spur us come let us fight.
With heart and with mind seeking truth and right
In a hallowed exalted morrow.

For this an hour of such bloodshed and strife.
With evils to darken and trouble life.
And no solace to find in dreaming.

50

But be we strong in the truth that we know.
Our minds will deal evil the final blow.
And men's madness succumb to reason.

So strong in faith let us fight as men.
For faith as 'tis written shall conquer when
In each heart it finds strength unfailing.

Formation: Circle with the Free Hold.
Steps: Open Ballad Steps. Walking Steps.
Rhythm: With faith to spur us come let us fight.
1   2   3   4   5   6   1-2

Bars.

Dance 2 open ballad steps and 4 beats of the next. On the   1—8
beats 3 and 4 the dancers stand still and slowly lower hands.   8 (—3—4)
The women step lightly into the ring as they stop and join
hands low at the sides.

The men join hands in like manner behind the women.

While singing: "In a hallowed exalted morrow":—The men 9—12
stand in place lifting arms SLOWLY inwards and upwards to
form arches, at the same time leaning body backwards and looking
upwards. The arms are lifted so slowly that they do not reach
the final arch position until the last word, "Morrow".   11—12
The arms should be straight but not stiff.

While the men are forming these arches the women take 2
quiet walking steps into the circle, Left. Right.   9—10

Standing on Right foot they make a Dropped Curtsey. (Place
Left foot on toe behind Right foot at the same time leaning well
back, looking upwards and lifting the arms SLOWLY inwards
and upwards. The Dropped Curtsey comes on the last word,
"Morrow". The women drop down so low that the Left knee 11—12
touches the ground.

In a ha	llowed ex	al	ted	mo	rrow.	9.10.11.12.
L		R		Down	-up	

51

Before beginning the next stanza hold the arms high for a little while. The context of this poem calls for slow singing and dancing to the music by Sparre Olsen.

BIBLIOGRAPHY

1. NORSKE FOLKEDANSAR I. Danseviser.
   (Songs and Ballads).

2. NORSKE FOLKEDANSAR II. Rettleiing om dansen.
   (Notated Folk-Dances with Illustrations).

3. NORSKE FOLKEDANSAR III. Slåttar til turdansane.
   (Airs to the Figure-Dance).

4. NORSKE FOLKEDANSAR IV. Danse-danse-dokka mi.
   (Song-Dances, Figure-Dances, Ring Games and Figure Games for Children and Young People).

(All these books are by Klara Semb).

5. NORSKE FOLKEVISER I LEIK OG DANS.
   (Norwegian Folk Songs in Games and Dances by Professor Olav Midttun).

6. DANSE, DANSE LETT UT PÅ FOTEN.
   (Folk dances, song-dances by Egil Bakka, 1970).

("Noregs Boklag", Oslo, have published all the above-mentioned books.)

7. NORSKE DANSETRADISJONAR. (Norwegian Dance Traditions) by Egil Bakka (Det Norske Samlaget, Oslo).

The following are of general interest:

"Ho tok oss med". (She Inspired Us.) An address to Klara Semb on her 80th birthday. (Noregs Boklag).

"Songdansen i Nordlandi." (The Song-Dance in the Nordic Countries by Hulda Garborg.) (H. Aschehoug & Co.)

"Idrett og Lek. Dans." (Sport and Games. Dance), in the series Nordisk Kultur (Nordic Culture).

52

NORSK ALLKUNNEBOK. (Encyclopedia of General Knowledge) (Fonna Publishers).

"Dances of Norway" by Klara Semb, in the series "Handbooks of European National Dances" (Crown Publishers, New York).

"Hardingfela" (The Hardanger Fiddle) by Sigbjørn B. Osa (Norwegian and English text).

"Norsk Folkemusikk" (Norwegian Folk Music) (Universitetsforlaget – University Press, Oslo). (Norwegian and English text.)

"The Story of Dance Music" by Paul Nettl (Philosophical Library, New York).

"– og fela ho lét" (The Hardanger Fiddle tradition) by Arne Bjørndal and Brynjulf Alver (Universitetsforlaget – University Press, Oslo). (With a summary in English.)

"The Norwegian Council for Folk Music and Folk Dance" – institutions and organizations in the Council, Norwegian folk dance and folk music, selected bibliography.

GRAMOPHONE RECORDS

In co-operation with the Norwegian State Broadcasting Company, recordings have been made of a selection of "Slåttar", "Stev" (Airs), and folk songs. All Norwegian folk music instruments are represented on these records. A series of recordings of music to the figure-dance, made by a figure-dance orchestra, is also available. All these records are on sale at music shops.

NOREGS UNGDOMSLAG

The Youth League of Norway was founded in 1896 and has now approximately 28,000 members. Its main object is to work for a general understanding and appreciation of the national values, and for fellowship and co-operation amongst young people. In 1965 the league had 33 county branches with approximately 900 individual clubs.

Some clubs have only folk dance on their programme, but most clubs offer additional activities.

Members of the Norwegian League of Youth meet every year in April/ May to discuss folk dance activities. Instructors and representatives from different branches of the organization express their views on policy and current issues.

Folk dance instructors have been in great demand during the last years. To meet this demand a two weeks' course is arranged every summer by the Norwegian League of Youth. The training provided at the courses is oriented to folk dance and aimed at instructors and youth leaders.

The local clubs arranged more than 1300 courses in folk dance in 1979, and 60 courses for instructors were offered under the direction of the district administration.

The Norwegian League of Youth distributes a publication, "Norsk Ungdom", to their members. Eleven issues of this paper appear yearly, and the column "Leikvollen" carries information about all kinds of activities arranged by the Norwegian League of Youth in the field of folk dance.

"Noregs Ungdomslag" is represented on the International Folk Music Council.
Its postal address is:
Noregs Ungdomslag
Kristian Augusts gate 14
Oslo 1